CALENDAR

by MYRA COHN LIVINGSTON

illustrated by WILL HILLENBRAND

Holiday House / New York

"Calendar" first appeared in *Wide Awake and Other Poems* by Myra Cohn Livingston,
illustrated by Jacqueline Chwast, and published by Harcourt, Brace and World, Inc.

Text copyright © 1959 by Myra Cohn Livingston
Illustrations copyright © 2007 by Will Hillenbrand
All Rights Reserved
Printed and Bound in China
The text typeface is Pink Martini Bold.
The illustrations were created using inks, acrylic, gouache, and collage on canvas.
www.holidayhouse.com
First Edition
1 3 5 7 9 10 8 6 4 2

Library of Congress Cataloging-in-Publication Data

Livingston, Myra Cohn.
Calendar / by Myra Cohn Livingston ; illustrated by Will Hillenbrand. – 1st ed.
p. cm.
ISBN-13: 978-0-8234-1725-4
ISBN-10: 0-8234-1725-5
1. Months–Juvenile poetry. 2. Children's poetry, American.
I. Hillenbrand, Will, ill. II. Title.
PS3562.I945C35 2007
811'.54–dc22
2006012145

To Josh
    M. G. L.

To all . . .
let us have hope
    W. H.

January
shivers,

February shines,

March blows off
the winter ice,

April makes the
mornings nice,

May is
hopscotch lines.

June is
deep blue swimming,

Picnics are July,

August is
my birthday,

September whistles by.

October is
for roller skates,

November is
the fireplace,

December is
the best because

of sleds

and snow

and Santa Claus.